Funny Bone Jokes

Ha-Ha Holiday JOKES to Tickle Your FUNNY BONE

Felicia Lowenstein Niven

Enslow Elementary

an imprint of

Enslow Publishers, Inc.

40 Industrial Road
Box 398
Berkeley Heights, NJ 07922
USA

http://www.enslow.com

Enslow Elementary, an imprint of Enslow Publishers, Inc.

Enslow Elementary® is a registered trademark of Enslow Publishers, Inc.

Library of Congress Cataloging-in-Publication Data

Niven, Felicia Lowenstein.
    Ha-ha holiday jokes to tickle your funny bone / Felicia Lowenstein Niven.
        p. cm. — (Funny bone jokes)
    Includes bibliographical references and index.
    Summary: "Includes jokes, limericks, knock-knock jokes, tongue twisters, and fun facts about Halloween, Thanksgiving, Christmas, Hanukkah, Kwanzaa, and other holidays, and describes how to create your own funny greeting cards"—Provided by publisher.
    ISBN 978-0-7660-3542-3
    1. Holidays—Juvenile humor. I. Title.
PN6231.H547N58 2010
818'.602—dc22

                              2010004193

Printed in the United States of America

122010 Lake Book Manufacturing, Inc., Melrose Park, IL

10 9 8 7 6 5 4 3 2 1

To Our Readers: We have done our best to make sure all Internet Addresses in this book were active and appropriate when we went to press. However, the author and the publisher have no control over and assume no liability for the material available on those Internet sites or on other Web sites they may link to. Any comments or suggestions can be sent by e-mail to comments@enslow.com or to the address on the back cover.

Every effort has been made to locate all copyright holders of material used in this book. If any errors or omissions have occurred, corrections will be made in future editions of this book.

♻ Enslow Publishers, Inc., is committed to printing our books on recycled paper. The paper in every book contains 10% to 30% post-consumer waste (PCW). The cover board on the outside of each book contains 100% PCW. Our goal is to do our part to help young people and the environment too!

Illustration Credits: © Clipart.com, a division of Getty Images, all clipart and photos.

Cover Illustration: Shutterstock.

Contents

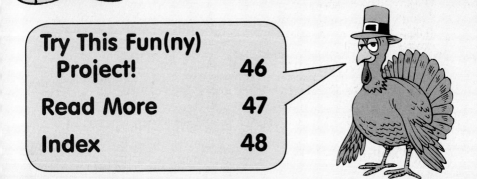

New Year's Eve/Day

What does the winner of the New Year's Day marathon lose?

His breath!

Why did the New Year's guest sit on a clock?

Because he wanted to be on time!

What did the digital watch say to the grandfather clock?

Look pop, no hands!

5

Midnight means many merry merrymakers.

Each time you see this squiggly box, it is a tongue twister! Try saying it five times fast!

Calendar countdown concludes with confetti!

Knock, Knock!

Who's there?

Abbott.

Abbott who?

Abbott time you made your New Year's resolution, isn't it?

6

FUN FACTS

Happy New Year! That greeting has been said for 4,000 years. It began back in Babylon. Then, New Year's parties were held in spring. They lasted for eleven days!

Times Square in New York City is a nice place for New Year's Eve. Thousands of people crowd together. They count down the final seconds of the year as a ball drops. It started in 1907. Back then, the ball was made of iron and wood. It had a hundred lightbulbs. It measured five feet and weighed 700 pounds. Today's ball is made of crystal. A computer controls it.

IT'S TRUE.

Yesterday always comes before today—or does it? Where is the place where yesterday follows today?

In the dictionary

As we dance away the night,
I can see a display of light.
A celebration
Across the nation
Oh, what a beautiful sight.

7

2 Valentine's Day

What do you call a very small valentine?

A valentiny!

What did the paper clip say to the magnet?

"I find you very attractive."

What did the stamp say to the envelope?

Stick with me and we'll go places!

A limerick is a funny poem that rhymes. Lines 1, 2 and 5 rhyme one way. Lines 3 and 4 rhyme another.

A tongue twister is a group of words with similar sounds. But try to say them fast. It's very hard to do.

IT'S TRUE.

There once was a woman named Mandy
Who thought Valentine's was just dandy.
Every person she'd meet
Said she was so sweet
That she could have been named Cotton Candy!

Knock, Knock!

Who's there?

Howard.

Howard who?

Howard you like a great big kiss?

Kathy's crunchy candy couldn't compare to Christy's caramel creams.

FUN FACTS

There are about one billion Valentine cards sent each year! Teachers get the most. Children also get a lot. Valentines are given to boyfriends and girlfriends. They go to husbands and wives. Pets even get them!

Watch out for Cupid! He might shoot you with a magical arrow. Of course, that's just a fun story. The Romans created Cupid. He is a boy with wings. He is the son of Venus, the goddess of love. Cupid's arrows made people fall in love. You will find Cupid on Valentine's cards and decorations. Just remember to duck. He might be pointing an arrow at you!

IT'S TRUE.

Loyal Leo longed to be lucky in love.

What letter adds value to a pear (and would be a good gift for Valentine's Day)?

The letter "L" makes pear into a pearl.

There once was a fellow named Art
Who was handsome, athletic, and smart.
A natural gourmet,
On Valentine's Day,
He made ham in the shape of a heart.

DID YOU KNOW?

Each holiday has its customs or traditions. These are the things that you do each time you celebrate. On St. Patrick's Day, one custom is to wear green. Another is to eat corned beef and cabbage.

IT'S TRUE.

Where would you find a leprechaun baseball team?

In the Little League!

Knock, Knock!

Who's there?

Warren.

Warren who?

Warren anything green today?

FUN FACTS

Shamrocks, or clovers, are fun on St. Patrick's Day. Sometimes they are lucky, too! Maybe you have a lucky clover. That's a clover with four leaves. Some clovers have more. But most clovers have three. It's hard to find the ones with more. You might have to look through ten thousand ordinary ones to find a lucky four-leaf clover!

IT'S TRUE.

Lucky leprechaun Larry likes lemon lollipops.

What do you get if you cross poison ivy with a four-leaf clover?

A rash of good luck!

Arbor Day celebrates trees. Earth Day reminds us we must care for the environment.

IT'S TRUE.

An evergreen tropical tree
Made of chocolate? I'm bouncing with glee!
It comes from it? Wow—
So I plant this cacao,
And there's even more chocolate for me?

Where can you find an ocean without water?

On a map

There once was a man named Gene
Who had an idea so keen
"I just have to say
We should have a whole day
Dedicated to making Earth green!"

FUN FACTS

You'll find the world's tallest tree in California. It is a giant redwood. It measures 379.1 feet. That is like a football field going straight up in the air. Only, the tree is a little longer. Another tall tree is the Ada tree of Australia. It reaches about 236 feet. Its roots like to stretch out. They can take up more than an acre of space.

IT'S TRUE.

Water winds westward where wild wildebeests wander.

Knock, Knock!

Who's there?

Ivanna.

Ivanna who?

Ivanna help the Earth, don't you?

5 Easter and Passover

Why do we paint Easter eggs?

Because it's easier than trying to wallpaper them!

Knock, Knock!

Who's there?

Hedda.

Hedda who?

Hedda marshmallow egg for you, but I ate it!

What ends the Passover Seder?

The letter R!

DID YOU KNOW?

You are part of a group of people. You share a common background. That means you are part of an ethnic group.

Not everyone believes in Easter. Not everyone keeps Passover. They are religious holidays. Whether or not you keep them depends on your faith.

IT'S TRUE.

Knock, Knock!

Who's there?

Howard.

Howard who?

Howard you'd like some matzo?

How many Easter eggs can you put in an empty basket?

Only one—after that it's not empty any more!

For Passover, I've given up bread.
That's something that some people dread.
But I don't mind one bit,
For you see, this is it.
I get lots of chocolate instead!

There was a young bunny named Jean
Who delivered her goodies unseen.
'Til the mailman one day
Found the spot where she lay
And collected her eggs, all fourteen.

How does the Easter
Bunny keep his fur neat?

With a hare brush!

The youngest at the table has a big job at Passover. He asks the Four Questions. Why is this night different from all other nights? The adults answer. They tell the story of the holiday. But they cannot finish without the hidden matzo or flatbread. It is called the afikomen. The child who finds it gets a prize.

IT'S TRUE.

Many mornings, mother mixed matzo meal.

What kind of cheese makes the best Matzo pizza?

Matzo-rella!

Six peeping chicks cheeping cheerily

23

DID YOU KNOW?

Are you patriotic? That means you love your country. In this case, it's the USA!

IT'S TRUE.

What did one flag say to the other flag?

Nothing. It just waved!

Proud police patrolled the patriotic parade.

Starred and striped soldiers strutted down the street.

At the start, to our feet we all sprang.
The Star-Spangled Banner we sang.
As we looked to the sky,
There arose a great cry,
And the fireworks began with a bang!

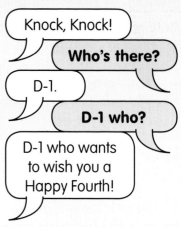

Knock, Knock!

Who's there?

D-1.

D-1 who?

D-1 who wants to wish you a Happy Fourth!

Independence Day brings celebration,
Hopefully you'll get the invitation.
Fireworks galore
Now guess what's in store?
Cheering throughout the whole nation!

FUN FACTS

Check this out. More than 66 million people cook out for the Fourth!

IT'S TRUE.

This coat comes in red, white, and blue but without buttons or zippers. How can that be?

It's a coat of paint.

What can you add to a cup of lemonade to make the drink disappear at a Fourth of July barbecue?

Holes

Knock, Knock!

Who's there?

Dozen.

Dozen who?

Dozen anyone want to see the fireworks?

What would you get if you crossed a patriot with a small curly-haired dog?

Yankee Poodle!

Halloween

7

What is in a ghost's nose?

BOOgers!

What do birds say on Halloween?

Trick-or-tweet!

Knock, Knock!

Who's there?

Ivan.

Ivan who?

Ivan to bite your neck!

What's orange on the inside and clear on the outside?

A pumpkin in a plastic bag!

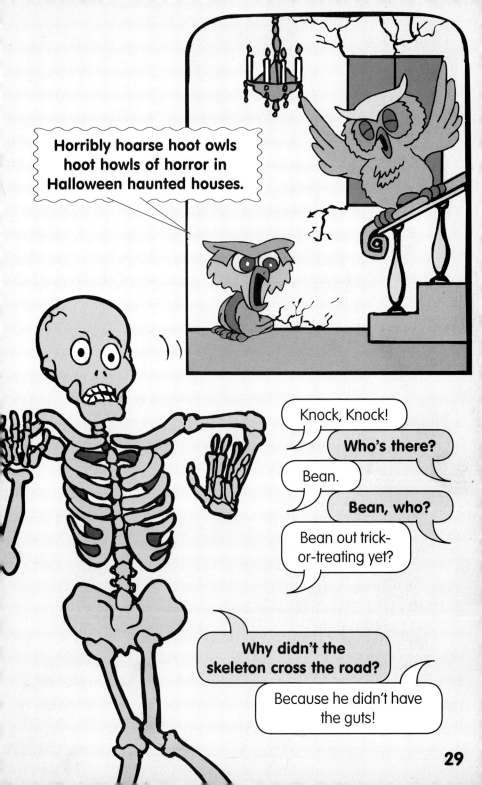

The finest achievement of man
Is candy, in bag, box, or can.
It's food just for joy,
A flavorful toy,
And dentists' retirement plan.

Transylvanian Tree Trimmers
are trained to trim the tallest
Transylvanian trees.

What is a mummy's favorite type of music?

Wrap

Though it's called "candy corn," I'm suspicious
Of this Halloween treat. It's delicious,
But as sure as you're born,
Though the name contains corn,
I suspect that it's not that nutritious.

If two witches would watch
two watches, which witch
would watch which watch?

What do you call a little monster's parents?

Mummy and Deady

FUN FACTS

Trick or treat! Halloween is big business! Each year, people spend about $2 billion just on candy. It is the largest candy-buying holiday. It is bigger than Christmas. It is bigger than Easter. It is even bigger than Valentine's Day! It is not just loved by kids. Most parents say that they sneak a treat from their kids' bags.

IT'S TRUE.

What sound does a turkey's phone make?

Wing, wing

What's the key to a great Thanksgiving?

A tur-key, of course!

Can a turkey jump higher than the Empire State Building?

Yes—a building can't jump at all!

DID YOU KNOW?

A national holiday is celebrated by everyone in the country. You are off from work and school. Thanksgiving is a national holiday. Black Friday, the day after Thanksgiving, is not—but many people do like to shop!

IT'S TRUE.

On Thanksgiving, there's plenty to do
Make the turkey, the side dishes, too.
When the family gathers round,
The very best sound
Is a happy Thanksgiving to you!

FUN FACTS

IT'S TRUE.

Thanksgiving is not just for Americans. Canadians have it too. But they celebrate it on a different day. In Canada, it is on the second Monday in October.

Knock, Knock!

Who's there?

Bacon.

Bacon, who?

Bacon a pumpkin pie—how about you?

Greedy gobblers grabbed the gravy.

There once was a turkey named Ben
Who lived in the farmer's large pen.
Though Thanksgiving was here,
Ben the turkey did not fear.
The farmer was a vegetarian—Amen!

Hanukkah and Kwanzaa

What did one candle say to the other candle?

Let's go out tonight!

Harmonic Veronica tried the Chanukah harmonica.

What did the wrapping paper say to the present?

I've got you covered!

Knock, Knock!

Who's there?

Abby.

Abby who?

Abby Hanukkah to you!

Knock, Knock!

Who's there?

Mayer.

Mayer who?

Mayer Kwanzaa be filled with peace and unity!

The holiday of Kwanzaa is here.
Its principles—all seven—are clear.
We work on unity, self-determination
Creativity, faith, cooperation
And more for the upcoming year.

I'm one more than half a dozen. Four less than eleven. I'm the number of Kwanzaa principles. My number is _____?

Seven

I'm shiny and hard. It's not easy to win. But on Chanukah, I love to take a spin. What am I?

A dreidel

FUN FACTS

When is Hanukkah? That is a good question! It might be in November. It could be in December. It could even be in January. It does not follow the regular calendar.

Hanukkah follows the Jewish calendar. It is based on the moon. The holiday begins four days before the new moon. This is a dark time.

Hanukkah, the Festival of Lights, brings light.

IT'S TRUE.

Knock, Knock!

Who's there?

Juno.

Juno who?

Juno what time it is? Time to light the candles!

Continue kinship by keeping Kwanzaa.

FUN FACTS

Do you know about Kwanzaa? It is based on an African harvest festival. Its name means "fresh fruits." Kwanzaa started in 1966. Today, it is known all over the world. The holiday lasts for seven days. It begins on December 26. It ends on January 1. Each day, candles are lit.

IT'S TRUE.

Patty patiently prepared potato pancakes.

The dreidel I made out of clay
Is ready for everyone to play.
It spins all around,
Without much of a sound.
Will it be Gimmel, Nun, Shin, or Hay?

What has wings, a long tail, and wears a bow?

A Hanukkah pheasant!

What kind of candle burns longer, a red candle, a green one, or a black one?

None. A candle always burns shorter!

How many people does it take to change a lightbulb at a Kwanzaa celebration?

None, there are candles not lightbulbs!

10 Christmas

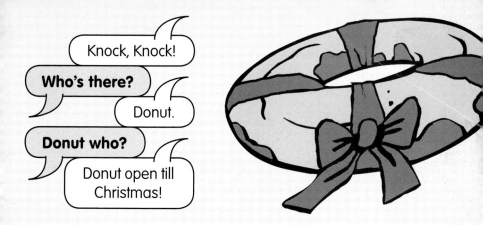

Pretty packages perfectly packed in paper.

FUN FACTS

Who has a very shiny nose? It's Rudolph! The reindeer came to life because of Robert L. May. He wrote the story. It was part of his job at Montgomery Ward. The store wanted a Christmas story they could give to their customers. Robert tested it on his four-year-old daughter. She loved it!

IT'S TRUE.

What do snowmen eat for breakfast?

Snowflakes!

A blizzard blew in Christmas Eve,
And just as St. Nick went to leave,
"That's great," Santa said,
"I'm off back to bed,
I can sleep late, I do believe!"

Try This Fun(ny) Project!

Now that you know a lot of new jokes, you can use them for more than laughs. Here is how to make your own funny cards.

WHAT YOU WILL NEED:

- this book
- construction paper
- markers and a pen
- glitter, ribbon, and other decorations (optional)

INSTRUCTIONS:

1. Choose a joke from the book. You might pick one for the holiday coming up.

2. Fold a piece of construction paper in half.

3. On the front of the paper, write the first part of the joke. Leave plenty of space for a picture.

4. Open the card. Write the answer to the joke on the inside. Leave space for more pictures and your name.

5. Now add your funny picture. You can decorate with glitter or ribbon if you like.

6. Write a happy holiday greeting and sign your name.

7. Your card is ready! Give it to someone who loves to laugh.

Read More

Books

Barbour Publishing. *Super Clean Jokes for Kids*. Uhrichsville, Ohio: Barbour Publishing, 2009.

Elliott, Rob. *Laugh Out Loud Jokes for Kids*. Ada, Mich.: Baker Publishing Group, Revell, 2010.

Phillips, Bob. *Good Clean Knock-Knock Jokes for Kids*. Eugene, Oreg.: Harvest House Publishers, 2007.

Weitzman, Ilana, Eva Blank, Rosanne Green, and Alison Benjamin. *Jokelopedia: The Biggest, Best, Silliest, Dumbest Joke Book Ever*. New York: Workman Publishing Company, 2006.

Internet Addresses

Jokes for Kids
  < http://www.activityvillage.co.uk/ kids_jokes.htm >

NIEHS Kids' Pages: Jokes, Humor, and Trivia
  < http://kids.niehs.nih.gov/ jokes.htm >

Index